Over Leveraging of Convenience

A Demise to Capitalism and Business

Kwasi Yeboah-Afihene

Copyright © 2014 by Kwasi Yeboah-Afihene

Library of Congress Control Number: Pending

ISBN-13:978-1505490961
ISBN-10:1505490960

All rights reserved. No part of this book may be reproduced or transmitted in any form or by any means, electronic or mechanical, including photocopying, recording, or by any information storage and retrieval system, without permission in writing from the copyright owner.

This book was printed in the United States of America.

      Author's contact details:

Kwasi_afihene@yahoo.com
Kwasi.afihene@gmail.com
[Also at: LinkedIn, Facebook and Twitter]

Dedication

This book is dedicated to the founding fathers of the UNITED STATES OF AMERICA and other Landmark leaders of the nation, Including President George Washington, President Abraham Lincoln, and President John F. Kennedy, and also all the other present and past leaders of the Nation, that has in their own efforts, preserved CAPITALISM to this date. Perfect or not, it is bigger than all of us.

Also to Adam Smith the father of classical economic who helped created the right environment to help us manage our ends, with the best of our efforts, to achieve happiness and well being. It is also worth mentioning great economists and business leaders of our contemporary times, who have dedicated their lives to preserve it, and also show the world the fruits of its workings, as well as its intricate mechanisms. These would include, Dr. Alan Greenspan, Dr. Ben Bernanke, Mr. George Osborne, Mr. William Gates and Mr. Warren Buffet, former Mayor Michael Bloomberg of NYC, Opera Winfrey, the basket ball legend Magic Johnson, and much more whom I may not have the chance to mention, but believe know themselves, and the enormous contributions they have made to this end. It is also worth mentioning the former Soviet Union Leader, Mr. Mikhail Gorbachev, for his introduction of the Perestroika, which was a workable hybrid of Capitalism and Communism in his Country, embracing the gems of Capitalism.

The last but not the least, my diseased father who believed in Capitalism, and also taught me as a student, to pay attention to what the Harvard Business Review says regarding business and economics. Then to all my surviving siblings, [Phyllis, Kwame, Kofi, Rita, Olivia, Kwaku, Akua, and Cornelia]

Thank you all for defending CAPITALISM, in your own little ways, and big ways, for I believe it is worth preserving.

OVER LEVERAGING OF CONVEVIENCE

[Demise to Capitalism and Business]

By

Kwasi Yeboah-Afihene

MAIN TOPIC

Over Leveraging of Convenience

[Demise to Capitalism and Business]

Preface

"The cycle of life is full of bitter and sweet experiences, most of which are unique, though some have quasi similarities. These cycles often stretch our human potentials exhaustively, and put us in situations that humble us, by showing the limitations of our human intellect and capacities.

The farthest stretch of our potentials sometimes yield very little results, and the amorphous nature of some of the issues leave as with very little clue as to even where to begin. Leaning on the providence of the divine, often serve us better, than over leveraging our own understanding alone.

This concept of "Over Leveraging of Convenience" could be a gem or menace. I will try to explain why, the best way I can.

Acknowledgements

I WILL SIMPLY GIVE THE GLORY TO GOD FROM WHOM ALL BLESSING FLOW, AND ALSO FOR PRESERCING CAPITALISM TO THIS DATE, TO BLESS THE ENTIRE WORLD.

Table of Contents

- Introduction
- From Our Humble Beginnings to How far we have Come
- Brief Basics of Micro-Economics: My Father's Wits
- Business Formation 101
- A bit of Macro Economics: My Father's wits
- The Geopolitical Environment in

which Free Market Capitalism thrives best

- A brief Description of the financial markets
- Convenience
- Over leveraging of Convenience at the Micro Economic Level
- Over leveraging of Convenience at the Macro Economic Level
- Overleveraging of convenience

and our state of health

- Conclusion

Introduction

There are two things about me that I have said repetitively, regarding my love for music, [all kinds of music that sooths my ears and love to enjoy], and also that I am a CAPITALIST. These statements are based on my confidence in its basic tenets. I believe with a very thoughtful implementation of these noble ideals, it will definitely do what it was designed to do, and much more.

Dr. Alan Greenspan, the most experienced and thoughtful economic philosopher of our contemporary times, gave a solemn caution, about the inner workings of the invisible hand, which works better, free of manipulations.

He has been repeatedly advising that, preserving free market capitalism in that fashion will serve us better. With his superior insights about the inner workings of free market capitalism, and life time devotion to perfecting its practice, I have no doubt about his assertions.

I hope he lives long enough, or leave a lot behind in writing, to help us all to benefit from his superior insights in the real practical inner working of CAPITALISM, and its pros and cons. Especially, what we should stress on in our practice, and what to shy away from in other not to undermine the purposes of its usage.

I say so because, the fruits of Mr. William Gates, Mr. Steve Jobs (late) and Mr. Warren Buffet, has benefited many. It has also driven the new direction of our global village. Some of their inventions provided the technologies that launched the momentum of globalization to the current speed of light. I say so, not because they have money. A lot of people also have money, and that is not why their names are worth noting in this introduction. The purposes for which they devoted their lives, knowing little about their ultimate outcomes, the apparent and hidden risks, are commendable.

I know so, because I have read a bit about them. How they started, their inner motivations, their life paths, and how it met opportunities that were impossible to discern in the beginning when they all started.

In New York City, where Dr. Alan Greenspan started in his chatter school, fiddling with mathematics and statistics, and latter getting excited about economics, little did he know where it would all end up.

Harvard is a great institution that everyone will be proud of holding their degree, not just sectional transcripts. If I were in Mr. Gates shoes, I would have completed, and have their degree. Mr. Gates found his purpose in life and passions much bigger than himself, and also all the other competing interests, and committed a life time of devotion to make it happen. What we are all witnessing with his great successes in both Microsoft, and most NOBLE philanthropic engagements via The Bill and Melinda Gates Foundation, is surely an example to mimic.

I believe the risks were insurmountable, especially at such a young age, with little experience to lean on, yet made such a judgment that turned out a superior choice, and benefited many. There are many more to acknowledge, but I would say that, the hills and valleys of life, is as little as oppose to the benefit of a genuine passionate desire to lead a purposeful life. Especially, with the heart of a servant, bearing fruits that benefits many people, either than ourselves alone.

At least, when I turn my laptop on and see the Microsoft Logo, it is Mr. Gates that comes to mind, though Microsoft is a company with its own identity. I would say, no matter what, stick with your convictions and passions, only if it is not too selfishly inclined. Even if, you do not live to see its fruits, your children, and children's children may come to at least see the tree, and in its season, also enjoy its fruits.

Mr. Steve Job's initial seed, did not serve him as well in the beginning, yet in the right season, where his genius in choreography and usability engineering became most needed, the fruit of his genius resurged.

Not that it was inferior in the beginning, yet the function of software was more of a pressing issue, than its form. His gadgets are more popular now, because at this stage in the evolution of technology, we can afford a little luxury, hence the preeminence of his most noble ideas. Though Mr. Gates, was right on the money from the word go, with the functionality of software being the most needed, Mr. Jobs, with patience and determined endurance, also did not turn out too bad. An early start or a late catch up, with patience, will get you somewhere. I say so, because Mr. Jobs also did not die broke.

Commitment, diligence, determination, focus, tenacity, courage, and of course, the divine energies that transcends our innate capacities, is what I have observed thrust most great men into stardom. These will include the founding fathers of this Great Country, the USA. Dreams come true, especially by the reliance on the latter.

There are many more who has similarly contributed as such in the past. To afford the younger generation the luxury of recognizing them without reading a history book, I will just add Mr. Ford, and the Wright Brothers who also made great strides in transportation, inventing the automobile and the air craft respectively. Their inventions also move people across the globe just as Mr. Gate and his contemporaries helped standardize software to not only improve business collaborative efforts, but also move data at the present speed of light, improving the efficiency of global collaborative engagements. These have helped globalization to flourish, and business to redefine its boundaries, without a humongous expense.

All those who perfected the development of the internet, to this date, companies the likes of; AT&T, Alcatel Lucent, Dell Computers, Apple Mac, Intel Corporation, Sysco Co, IBM Co, and also all the thought leaders in the Insurance and Finance Industry; Allstate Insurance Co, State Farms Insurance Co, J. P. Morgan Chase Bank, City Group, Goldman Sacs, Bank of America,

Lloyds Bank, Deutsche Bank, Barclays Bank, Bank of Canada, Standard Charted Bank, Bank of China, and all others in the insurance and banking community deserves a praise. Their efforts to create the right environment and also the liquidity needed to sustain businesses all over the world, with a very efficient and effective risk management systems, is not only essential, but of critical essence.

Mr. Warren Buffet's contribution regarding the best and most sustainable ways to invest, rather than following bubbles, with his "Bufferttology" concept and philosophy of investing is also a formidable contribution. This has deep insights and wisdom, regarding the gems of thoughtful investments, with long term benefits, with sustainability as a guideline, instead of the rush to pursue quick riches. Mr.

Buffet, has not just talk about this, he has also proven it, with his life and actions, which has evidently shown in the value of his conglomerate, Berkshire Hathaway.

There are a lot more people to thank for their contributions in other nations, that I may not know about, but I cannot forget also the wits and guts of the British business mogul, Sir Richard Branson, the founder of the Virgin Group. There may be more elsewhere, as I have said earlier, but will end it here. The contributions of these great men, which will transcend them, and will even live after them to benefit us all and posterity, is worth noting.

To all of the people around the globe, regardless of their economic philosophy, and local political structures within their individual sovereign nations, we are all favorably incline to some of the fruits of CAPITALISM. Be it a communist nation, a populist or a socialist nation. The legacies of Capitalism, transcends our individual ideological differences, as I have already highlighted.

I can go on and on and on, but will save the rest, for the main body of the book, and will not bore you so much with an unending introduction. I will therefore say, as you will all agree with me, that the brain children of these ideas, as well as those who made its superior values and benefits so visible, deserve the right recognition. Many more have been left out, though not purposefully. I am hopeful that you would pardon me, and give yourselves a pad in the back. To say God bless you all, is the least we can do, in earnest prayer, wherever they are.

I however still think it need a bit of tweaking, though not much needed, except a little improvement in its implementation, especially in their adaptations in specific geopolitical systems. It is definitely worth preserving, and I believe you will all agree with me.

From Our Humble Beginnings to How far we have come

The example I am going to use in this section may have some religious connotations, inclined to the Christian Faith. However the relevance of the analogy has not much to do with it. I am using it as an example to shed more light on what I am about to say. Christian or not, I still believe it does not change the principles being highlighted here.

It is the story of Adam and Eve and their family. They had two children, the eldest of whom was Cain and the younger Able. One was a farmer, and the other was a shepherd. From what we know about history those were the most prominent jobs available at the beginning of times, in almost all cultures. If there is anyone who knows any different, I believe it will be worth sharing. There was a time that they had to sacrifice some of the fruits of their labor. The shepherd gave up his best produce for the sacrifice, and the farmer, used the not so fresh produce for his. As the story goes, the shepherd's sacrifice was accepted, because he gave the best of himself and the outcomes of his labor. The farmer also did his best, yet not all he could do. And his sacrifice was not well accepted.

The acceptance of the former's gift triggered a jealous rage in the other. The outcome was somewhat dismal, yet God chose based on the extent of the sacrifice each other made. It is therefore worth going an extra mile in all pursuits, irrespective of the apparent positive or negative nuances. Just keep on pressing on, with all good purposes and intents, and live the rest to God and time. Sometimes we may not live to see the outcomes of the seeds we sow, yet if it is expected to bear good fruits, it will definitely benefit those we leave behind, who will be there when the fruits ripen.

As the population of the world grew a bit more, we advanced in our methods for feeding ourselves, improving agricultural techniques that used farm animals to till the land, improving our productivity and resource efficiency. This was a very convenient way of leveraging our land to feed ourselves, and other resource to help us meet our ends.

Depending on the agricultural pursuits of interest, and the vegetation the local terrains afforded, animal husbandry also became a little more advanced. With very little advancement in the renewable techniques of vegetation, people moved around to save themselves and their cattle and sheep and so on. With these animals being their most important form of wealth, they did everything to preserve it in order to sustain themselves and family for the present and the future.

Life stock formed the bulk of the "estate" they leave behind for posterity. In those days, such elements of the estate of the head of the family, was the most cherished. The migration of such families with these kinds of legacies became very essential for its preservation. Nomadic life style for such families became very common.

This same movement or migration prevented them from owning land to till. As such they traded a bit with their meat, for produce that the locals who own enough land to farm also produced. Essentially that was the beginning of trading, [The Butter Trading] which eventually evolved into our current levels and sophistications in commerce. In its intricate complexities in our contemporary times, things have not changed much. A lot of products were added from natural resources, which also made the trading a bit more complex. As this kept growing with time, it became a bit difficult to carry produce around for gold or silver, or even shoes and cloths, if you do not have the skill and resources to do them yourself.

The evolution of such trading with natural resources that was needed for consumption or the production of other durable and non durable consumables, is what eventually grew into the commodities market. I have taken a quantum leap from where I began the story to this end.

It however, did not get here that fast. In between were other commonly accepted mediums, which helped to ease the burden of moving things around in exchange for what others needed, that they do not have themselves. The process started very slowly with cola in some cultures, and many other variations of acceptable mediums of exchange for trading conveniences. This was the onset of the evolution of currency, which's purpose was to make commerce and trading convenient, as well as the processes that were used to produce the related merchandize. In effect, it is a tool and a reward. Markets, where various merchants met to trade their products also grew in varying complexities.

In the small communities societies started to evolve, there were not many activities in general, including trading, hence business was very simple. The elements of the weather, which sometimes were so cruel to communities, hampering the progress of their noble economic pursuits, force them to also move around.

Such movements engendered the need for some to cohabit with others, who had been so fortunate to be spared by such unfavorable weather elements. They lived together graciously and peacefully in the pursuits of their individual ends. This also complicated some of the norms of the cultures. Hybrid cultures began to form.

The geographical elements, and resources the inhabitants of the land, were endowed with, was the main saving grace for their survival. This then engendered the need in the development of the initial economic philosophies, to emphasize the preeminence of the Land, as the main factor the wealth of nations depended on. This idea was most embraces by the "physiocrats".

It carried the world for a very long time, and had its gems also, though was transient. It served its generation so well, and it was good, in its time. Its proponents also deserve some accolades for helping to carry a generation to at least the end of its usefulness. It was the best way in its times, for one to manages their ends, and for that purposes, it did so well.

I will not bore you with a lot of detailed economic philosophical precepts, for that is not the main purpose of this book. I just wanted us to have a little understanding of how it all began, and grew so complex with time. The explosion of local populations necessitated a more effective and productive ways of satisfying our needs and managing our ends efficiently.

These complexities and all its intricate nuances are what ultimately necessitated the theories and models in classical economics. The world struggled with the best ways to manage our ends for quite a while. As I said before, sometimes our ingenuous ideas may not be trash as such, but may just need some time, for the systems and structures within our confines to spot its usefulness

Mr. Gates' perseverance through time and Mr. Jobs' patience with time, all paid off. At least the gadgets we are all holding in our hands today, the IPhone and the rest of others, all makes this point so visible, and does not need much more emphasis. I grew up with the walkman, and eventually, the windows. I do not mean the house door or window, but I hope you still get my point. It was quite an exciting journey through time and history, and I do not want to bore anyone with some of them, especially those that do not add much value to where we are going with this.

It was right at the onset of the industrial revolution, which was after the World War II, that the complexities of production and its right labor mix lost the flea for the economic philosophy at those times. As necessity dictates the inventions and innovations in all spheres of life, history raised another hero, to help shape the ideas that propelled us to the next stage.

In our times, this was the great classical economist and moral philosopher Mr. Adams Smith. His most thoughtful piece of writing, which has been perfected in its evolution to help the world manage our ends to this date, is his famous book, "The Wealth of Nations", in short. It helped redefine the most essential elements of production and other means of generating the wealth of nations to help provide the needs of its people.

The main philosophical and ideological difference between the old and new was to shift our focus from the land alone as the most important factor in the generation of the wealth of nations, and leverage our human capacities and gifts, for that is a superior resource to earn us better returns in our quest for managing our ends, in pursuit of our well being and happiness.

The shift in the models and theories regarding classical economics as we know today, started from this central paradigm shift. Had it been so forcefully resisted by society, I do not know what better economic philosophy could have guided us to date.

The structures of governance needed with the appropriate administrative complimentary structures, markets and industries to drive us along, was a challenge for a very long time. It is hard to say, yet time has only given us two polar ends with a couple of variations in between.

They say, or some say, there are no absolutes. Absolutes or not, is not the most important, though in some situations there are. As there is the Sun and the moon, and all the rest of our celestial bodies, which keep us warm and give us light we can absolutely refer to them. For their exact positions however, some astronauts may have an idea, where the moon resides. For the sun, I do not know if we have been that daring yet. Touching the sun or the moon physically is not even what matters, if all you need is a little bit of warmth and light.

What really matters in my opinion is your inclination toward the direction of the moon or the sun. A favorable positioning will definitely provide the light and warmth needed. I will definitely not go to Antarctica, if warmth is what I need, or light. Simply, you may not have the luxury of enjoying much of it, as sparingly as they are most naturally endowed.

This is just a metaphor, yet with a deep insight as to our philosophical inclinations regarding the guidelines and boundaries needed to afford us the flexibilities we need to manage our end, as a society, a county or even our global village. The forces of nature has brought us this far, and it will be a misnomer to even attempt to turn the tide.

Whether, we curse Mr. Gates and his folks, or Dr. Greenspan for his ingenious passion for free market capitalism, or Mr. Buffet for his enthusiasm, for showing us how it should be harnessed, tides are not easily pushed around. We just have to go with the flow and manage our apparent risk and future perceived.

Whiles we monitor very critically its direction, at least to make sure we do not lose our way, the purposes of all of this is not in its mechanics, but the ultimate pursuit of happiness and well being for all. If we lose sight of that, and get too busy with the process, without paying attention to our destination. It will be like a plane in the air without radar to steer it in the right direction toward the right destination. It will be OK if you have an affinity for high altitudes, but you can only stay there as long as you want, only if you have either an infinite amount of fuel or a filling station up there, which I am not sure of any that is suspending in the air. If the end or destination is why we took off, then we need to steer carefully to the right landing field. Anywhere else, may warrant us to take off again. If we land at a local airport, with the wrong or inappropriate run way, it will be difficult to run and we may be stuck there.

We therefore have to be very careful in steering the radar in the right direction with a more accurate GPS. A GPS though is a tool which can only get you where you are going, if you know exactly where, and direct it as appropriate. The rest is monitoring the other nuances that can force a deviation carefully, with the destination in mind to avoid getting lost in the woods. You can also enjoy the luxury of a balloon air ride, which often stand still. If a vacation is what made you fly to see the aerial view of your surroundings, that may also be in order.

I do not know anyone at the airport, who doesn't know where they are going. Even if it is interstate, or intrastate, the distance does not matter, so long as you are sure of where your plane is intended to land. Off the airport, you will then finally go home, your business, or whatever purpose which necessitated the travel. If it was just an expedition, it's also well and good, so long as you are sure of why you chose that destination.

Brief Basics of Micro-Economic: My Father's Wits

Economics is classified as a social science. There are a lot of definitions out there with varying flavors, most of which describe the concept well enough. I will however use a very simple definition which is easy to relate to. This definition was introduced to me by my father, who introduced me to business and the capitalist doctrine as a student. He was not an economist, just a business man. He however had very deep insights about the economic environment which his business resided.

He was a manufacturer and was in fact the first person to introduce "Mattress" to Ghana. He also introduced a lot of things most of which helped Ghana in implementing their boarding secondary school systems. He introduced the steel trunk which most Ghanaian students used for packing their school items to enable them to conveniently survive on campus. He also introduced the bunk beds, which most students slept on. He had an excellent distribution system which included retail and wholesale distribution outlets. He also had contracts with the Ministry of Health and Education, supplying their respective institutions with related products.

He supplied most of his products to these institutions on credit till they managed to pay him back, so that the schools could be run effectively without destructions, regardless of their ability to secure leverage to meet payments for their invoices. Unfortunately, some of these receivables ended up being bad debt, especially for the schools in the very remote area.

He started business very early in life and worked very hard to establish it. Hard work, focus, dedication, determination, tenacity, and above all the love to live for a purpose that is bigger than himself were his prime mantra and most apparent tenets. He was definitely sustained by the providence of the divine, which guided him to succeed.

He learnt most of the skill he brought to Ghana from the Great Britain. He indeed did very well for himself, and also helped many others through his work and products. He was once the chairman of the Ghana Chamber of Commerce, and shared a lot of capitalist ideas with young entrepreneurs who were starting off. His favorite business reading was the Harvard Business Review which was even difficult to get in Ghana then.

He had affiliations with a lot of international business folks, including some from the United Kingdom, and the USA. This may not be relevant to Micro Economics, but I just introduced my father, simply because most of what I am going to share may not be text book ideas only, but what I learnt from him, coupled with that from college in Ghana, [The University Of Ghana – Legon], as well as NJIT and Rutgers University.

These are some of his ideas of business and business formation as they relate to Micro economics. He said the basic units of micro economics are suppliers who produce goods and services, as well as retailer and wholesalers who distribute. Most suppliers are either manufactures, resellers or big manufactures in manufacturing units, which are mostly called factories. The main idea is to use raw and intermediate materials to produce outputs, which are products and services in the most efficient way, harnessing labor and other resources to ultimately make some profit after selling their respective outputs. The level of efficiency, in the usage of both labor and material is what often improves the bottom line, given a good lid on operational expenses. If you keep things tight enough, controlling waste, you will be OK. Even better, if you are able to sell and collect most of your receivables.

If you manage the end to end process well, you are most likely going to improve your odds. He also told me that, in the course of doing business, there are a lot of things that you may not be able to control. These things he said could bring the business down. I then asked him, in that case what do you do? He said you need business or commercial insurance. If you have the right coverages, they will serve you well, providing the appropriate indemnification in a rainy day. In fact he was the one who thought me for the first time, what indemnification really meant, in terms of insurance claims regarding such business losses. There are a lot more he said regarding the production side of business.

He then also explained to me, how the retail side of business works, especially how to price merchandise with appropriate mark-up to still be OK, given your administrative and other operational expenses. He explained price variability within seasons to improve merchandise turn around as well, in a way to still make some buck. He very well understood business relationships and did very well for himself as a result. He established good business contacts with both public and private individuals, and other stakeholders.

In spite of his success in business, he was very humble. In fact, it was his humility that attracted many to him. That was one of his traits that drew a lot of important personalities to him. He had friends in both high class societies as well as low. He did not judge people by their social or socio-economic class. He was approachable by a wide variety of individuals from all walks of life.

He once told me, sometimes circumstances in life gets you in a hole which is smaller than your physique. It is humility that often does it. He then cautioned, never let anyone trample on you with disrespect. That is not humility. He said also, that I do not to be ashamed of doing anything productive and ethical to survive, when situation call for it, because it is just temporary.

Never give up your dreams, but trust God. If you keep on going, you will get further along, at least from where you started. In fact, it was this advice that helped me to start my PhD program, for which I have come a bit further from where I started given the challenges, with the help of God.

I will tell most of the young folks to trust God, and also listen to the advice of your more matured adults around them. It may not be relevant today or tomorrow, but who knows?

On the consumer side, he also spoke about how to expose your value proposition to your targeted audience, through your marketing efforts. For business to business transactions, relationship building with respective stakeholders, he said was the most formidable tool.

These he said, in his case, included government and private institutions and other businesses. He also mentioned, contract negotiations with such institutions, and how realistic and achievable expectations are needed to be set and managed. Getting his PO [Purchase

Order] cut quick enough, in payment of respective invoices was also very critical him. He said this was very essential in avoiding dad debts and eventual insolvency. He said many things about business to me, including the fact that, the most important marketing tool was integrity, and the cheapest, a genuine smile.

He said as a joke, integrity is sometimes harder to develop than a real honest smile. If your hand shake means the same all year round, you will be OK. Because most people frown on chameleon handshakes, which he explained by simply saying, just be disciplined and principled. Do not have a wavering thought. Be thoughtful, yet stick with your convictions. If you believe it, pray about it and kept your focus straight. If it is the will of God, it will be OK.

In fact, one of the things he told me from the last time I saw him, was simply this; in your journey of life, just trust God and he will get you wherever he is sending you. Just tick with your convictions and let God. He was a bit frail, and in my opinion had lost a bit of his cognitive sharpness, as compared to how I knew him. I noticed a bit of memory lapses in our conversation, as well as others previously.

He also explained a bit to me, about the other most important pieces of micro economics. He said, families and individuals form the consumer base, which mostly supports most businesses. They roam in different market places to find what are needed to meet their ends. Some of these may be food, clothes, shoes, and so on, and of course, a mattress to sleep on at night. That in fact is where I come in, to help people sleep well at night so they can get up again and go to work the next day, or do whatever they set off to do.

These families he said, have limited resources that may not meet all their needs. They therefore have to choose what they need most, and can afford to buy with the money they have. They decide what to use the money for, base of what is most important to them or the family. The best choice often is what is deemed most valuable, or what has a superior opportunity cost. In fact I have been throwing that around in most of my writings; at least at this point you know where I got it from.

My father did not attend a formal business school. He learnt mostly by doing, and self learning through business materials like the

Harvard Business Review and some others. He read a lot of related business articles from reputable magazines and journals, and informally tutored himself, with the help of other mentors and friends. His business acumen was partly genetics, and also, getting his feet on the street early in life.

I threw in genetics because his father was also very business minded with very little formal education as well. They both did well, I would say. He also said, it is good to live for a purpose, not convenience alone. For convenience only come after a purpose well served and lived. It does not precede it. If you put it in the wrong other, it may not serve you well in life.

In fact, this was what sewed the seed that geminated into the idea of overleveraging of convenience, especially the distractive ends it can potentially bring. In fact he was a capitalist just as I am, yet he was cautious of overleveraging anything, especially those with destructive impetus. He was well misunderstood by many, because of his "stubborn" loyalty to his conviction, and focus to achieve his goals in business and any others he puts his eyes on. With the help of God, most of them materialized.

      Our local markets in Ghana were not as big. If we had the expanse of markets as in the USA, or if globalization was initiated in his era, with the boundless market expansions it affords local businesses, I bet he could have been the like of any business mogul anywhere. The only restriction was the local nature of his business, with a very restrictive and structured niche market.

I have not touched on everything there is to know in Micro Economics, but I just chose to share a bit of my father's business practical wits. I hope it will help many in combination with the formal economic theories that we learn in school. What I shared with you, is just feet on the street economics from my father, with little refinements from his informal business readings. In other words it is mostly practical. That is all that did it for him, with the rest of his own innate capacities and reliance on God. Though he was not that pious as others may prefer him to be, yet was true to himself.

As much as the family is the most formidable axiomatic element of the consumer base of the micro economic model, so are businesses big and small. Businesses however are born out of ideas of thoughtful men and women, who commit bravely to the purposes God illumines in their hearts and minds, which ignites their passions to help solve problems in their societies, countries and the whole world, as Mr. Gate's example is a good one, so is Ms. Opera Winfrey, and all the noble entrepreneurs all over the world. I say noble, because the inherent risks of business incubation and nurturing to maturity does not take an individual innate capacities alone to succeed. . I believe there is an element of the providence of the divine. Sometimes, it may not seem that way, but the ways of God are beyond our understanding.

To encourage all entrepreneurs, and will be entrepreneurs, young and old. Do not throw out your passions, or noble ideas God has put in your hearts, as well as gifts you are endowed with. Everyone's gifts are different, just as our

DNA. For all you know, there may be only one of you anywhere, and loosing those God given natural endowments, may deny not only yourself, but posterity the chance to even polish it and enhance it to make their lives better.

Moses was the only one who received the Ten Commandments for Jehovah. It was however meant for all. With anger, he was also the only one, who broke it all at ones. That I will say was the record, for breaking the Ten Commandments. Grace is why we are all here, and nothing else. For every one break them also, but at least not all at ones.

Whatever you are endowed with, just be patient, and not let anger destroy it for everyone, nor lack of courage. It is he who defends his own work, and he gives ownership to whoever he pleases. You could say, Mr. Gates was a college drop out. That may be then, but now his inventions are part of what is propelling us to the next era. Just do not give up, unless it is absolutely impossible beyond all odds. However, these odds have little to do with our personal resources and capacities, which often can be over stretched with the help of God.

Stick in there and it will be OK. Microsoft will thrive and so are all small businesses, the likes of; Riteez at the Willowbend Mall in Dallas TX. I will however caution though that, sometimes like Jonah, it is the will of God that is ultimately done. If you accidentally and even willfuylly lose your way, he get you back in the direction of his will.

I will give you an example, but not in detail, since the intricate details are not necessary, to prove my point. All I am trying to say is that, if a life venture fails to work against all odd, maybe it is an expedition, or an exploratory journey to lean more in preparation for more meaningful and purposeful ventures. After my career with AT&T, I tried several ventures.

From RAC & JAY Inc, which I named after my children, and RAC & JAY Health Services which became an off shoot from that. I also founded, Afihene Financial Group which worked so well, yet sold it, when business and economic tensions surged beyond my capacity to word them out during a terrible economic near depression conditions, during which leverage to small businesses also became temporarily extinct. This forged a dismal current ratio for most entrepreneurs, and even more so for those in the financial and insurance industry, due to unfavorable industry wide business cycle. I decided to go back to school after I sold the business.

This though seemed like a sad story, I did not see it that way, because of my confidence in the capitalist system in which I lived. In that environment, I knew very strongly that God and life is all that is needed, because he has never fails to redeem himself. Through all the changes of life, in trouble and in joy, he said, make you his service your delight, and he will make your wants his care.

I borrowed money here and there to to add to my resources to survive school. By the grace of God I am know a PhD candidate, currently working on my Dissertation.

The long story short, as brook as I became as a student, all that was left was my laptop, with no sophisticated publishing application, than just what we are all familiar with, even in high and elementary schools. My laptop was even broken and had to handle it diligently and carefully. I held it like gold, because if it had broken then, it would have been difficult to replace.

The application was Microsoft Office. I only used, word and PowerPoint, not even the most sophisticated one, like Publisher, though I had it as well.

My first book was written, when I was working at night during my first semester in college. There was no desk, yet with my laptop on my lap, and with no internet to even draw much from any other sources, the grace of God was sufficient. Working hard at it, between work and home, I come up with my first book, and also a 4.0 GPA, which I maintained till date, since I am already a candidate and has no more courses to take.

I have passed my qualifying exams which has afforded me the luxury to produce my academic contributions. By that I mean the body of knowledge or domain for which I believe will help me start my next journey. There may be a lot more to say, yet not necessary for the point I am trying to make.

Believe what God has said about your life, and perceiver no matter what, for he can even turn bankruptcy, or a penny less piggy bank, into something unimaginable. Take chances and mitigate your risks well. Do not give up, stick with your dreams, and work toward it a day at a time, for that is all you have.

Pray also, for meeting the right opportunity that will propel you to your final destination. Chance can happen to anyone. Your odds can definitely be improved by the favor of God on your life. His favor however is by grace, and faith has a lot to do with it. It takes faith to have the needed patience to let grace work in God's terms, not necessary ours.

As I said, it takes both big and small businesses to keep the micro level of any economy working and doing well. The big have the tentacle to be flexible, they are a formidable force in the mix, and so are small businesses. Though the latter, expends more physical and emotional energy, as well as a higher risk. If you truthfully believe in your dreams, go all out and do not give up.

No matter how young or old your business is, if you nurture it well, it will grow and mature with time. Perseverance and hard work will get you somewhere. The fear of failure, which stifles your own momentum and engenders an unwarranted inertia, can even get you sick due to inherent sedentary lifestyle resulting from inaction. Whiles working hard, will do you better, health wise as well as financially, and affords you lots of freedom. Working for free or for money or even waiting patiently for deferred gratification as most business start-ups demand, will improve the same odds. This is true though, if you can keep a level head not succumb to the flow of emotional tides, that could get you the same place Moses was, though God being so gracious, gave him a second chance, which he most prudently handled and delivered cautiously to his people.

Though I am not out of the woods yet, with my laptop fully functional, and Microsoft Office alone, I have produced almost thirty one volumes currently being distributed by Amazon.com. These though include both paper back and electronic versions. Some of the books even have Spanish translations.

We will all leave this earth for one reason or the other. The reason does not really matter much. The most important is the purpose for which you life for or die, for both are eminent. If he blesses you with life, live it purposely, not only conveniently. Though there is nothing wrong with enjoying some conveniences life affords.

A purposeful life will definitely afford you some conveniences, that are more enjoyable, and can also afford you a good night's sleep, as well as needed energy for the day's work. Entrepreneurship is not a walk in the park, but fortunately or unfortunately there is no way or any other way to leading a successful life, either than making meaningful scarifies with very serious commitment, and manage the associate risks with caution trusting God.

I will end this chapter with a quote from our president and one of our well known celebrities, The Actor Tom Hanks.

President H. Barack Obama:

"Focusing your life solely on making a buck shows a poverty of ambition. It asks too little of yourself". The rest of this quote is in one of my books, the little Blue Inspirational Series Vol. III on page 32.

The actor Tom Hanks *also said this differently:*

Help Publicly, Help privately. Help in your actions by recycling and conserving and protection, but help also in your attitude. Help makes sense where sense has gone missing. Help bring reason and respect to discourse and debate." The rest of this quote is also in the same book quoted above on the next page. Page 33.

Business Formation 101

A seed is what geminates into a plant or a tree. When you grow a seed, you would never know how tall of a plant or a tree you will eventually end up with. The only thing you know for sure is the kind of tree you expect. You cannot grow an oak tree to expect a mango tree out of it.

You may not know, how tall of a mango tree you would get eventually, but if you sew a mango seed, you will definitely come up with either a mango plant or a tree. Whether your seed end up a plant or a tree depend on you, the natural vegetation of the region, and the conditions of the soil. All things being equal, your choice will depend on the purpose for cultivating the seed. The main motivation for sewing a seed however is the purpose for which its fruits are intended to be used.

It is not so easy to get to the maturity stage of the fruits. It takes work, and a lot of it. There is a natural way the mango tree grows. For any plant, with the right sunshine, natural rain or manual delivery of water, carbon dioxide, and weeding a little at a time, it will geminate and grow naturally. The right mix of these will trigger the internal working of the plant, like photosynthesis and all the other related mechanism that precipitates its growth to get you the natural size of the tree, given its own genetic composition and predispositions.

The last point though has a lot to do with our vision and mission. For example, Mr. Gate's vision was a million time bigger than his father's garage, yet Microsoft in an ocean in its own rights, far bigger than the garage of the biggest mansion in the world. I do not know where Sir. Richard Branson started exactly.

I only started following him a bit, during the virgin records days, prior to the Virgin Atlantic Airlines. I do not know how big the Virgin Group is at the moment, but from its size in the market, I do not think he can either rival Berkshire Hathaway or Microsoft. Just a little joke to Sir Richard, I know you are also an ocean in your own rite, which is equally formidable. The only thing I think Mr. Gate cannot even try to compete with you, is probably your guts, though he may be trailing closely.

A business idea as compared to a vision, is sometime like a pin drops. The idea however should serve a pain, or a purpose, for which you are most passionate and well endowed to pursue. It also has to be a pain for enough people, who are willing and is able to pay you the appropriate price for your service. The worse the pain is to them, the more they will be willing to pay for your solution. It is not just a matter of enthusiasm. There has to be a need for your products and services, and also an audience with the ability to pay for it.

The rest is how you organize your resources to make it happen in the most efficient way. If you keep on pressing on, with a little leverage here and there from wherever you can get it from initially, a responsible use and efficient mix of the resources will get your product reasonably competitive, and turn out a little decent return.

Recycling the extra return back into the business here and there, focusing on your growth plan, and market share expansion strategy, with a keen eye on the external economic and political environment, you could navigate the land mine pretty well. Being able to afford enough liquidity and a reasonable current ratio to maintain the right cash flow to keep you going, could win you success with patience and time. With a restrictive current ratio, you may potentially face cash flow problems, which could be a treat to your survival

The challenges of business along its path is insurmountable, but so long as you have enough mix of cash and resources to sustain your operations, yourself and family with even bread and water, you will be OK eventually, if you are lucky to meet the right chance-base opportunity, that can accelerate your momentum. Be it a technology accelerator or intellectual property based competitive advantage, or an awesome innovation, which gives you an edge in the market place.

Some of these things, you just have to keep a hawks eye in your business environment and watch the trends very carefully. Most often your eye may connect with your vision, and with a little pollen in the environment, things could pollinate in a way you may not even imagine.

I do not think Mr. Zuckerberg had an idea where Facebook would be, when he started. So is Miss Opera Winfrey. Chance can happen to anyone who dares to try. The rest is God, who really makes it all happen, if you do not give up.

A bit of Macro Economics: My Father's wits

The macroeconomic environment is mainly the aggregation of the various elements and outputs of the production systems and consumer bases within a geo-political environment. All what this means, in simple terms is that, the output of individual industries and businesses within a particular country, and their consumer bases, modeled with the fundamental economic theories and philosophy. This eventually precipitates into two major curves, with opposing dynamic movements, which are influence by price and quantity.

These dynamic movements of the aggregate demand and supply curves, simplistic as it may seem is intricately very complex. Some of the complexities are modeled well in the curves and other econometrics models. It is however so complex that it cannot possibly be completely modeled. As a result of that, there is a very huge abstraction that is assumed to be constant, therefore creating a big black box, with a lot of inherent uncertainties.

These uncertainties are what sometimes make or unmake a business if caught unaware. It is therefore incumbent on any business leader to keep a hawk's eye on their business environments in other not to be blindsided by some of these nuances.

Leaving it up to chance alone, though you may not understand it all, could be very catastrophic. With today's technology, related business data can reveal a lot of information that can provide important actionable-insights that can help guide business decisions that could improve their odds, and help them mitigate some of the blind spots in the maze. In economic theory, some refer to it with the phrase; "All things being equal", though it is really a misnomer. All things can never be equal. Not so much as in individual rights, but our natural endowments and experiences.

The inclination of our gifts and natural endowments, our affinity for financial freedoms and others, only calls for a natural variability. All things therefore, cannot be equal, especially within different, domains. The domains themselves are also different. There is therefore a very invaluable need for flexibility and reasonable accommodations to different perceptions as they relate to the reality on the table.

Trust is what breaks the wall to even start any dialogue. You cannot tell a roster to bark because you are a "chiwawa", simply because rosters are rosters, and they do not bark. They can however collaborate well on common interest andmutually beneficial issues. An employer and employee relationship is base on the same principle.

The employer may be absorbing an uncertainty for the employee, yet the employee's intellectual property which are patentable, equally absorbs business uncertainties. It is therefore import that we respect each other. Harmony and peace is what create the right synergy and environment to collaborate.

Overleveraging ones card, may sooth our ego, but not progress in business or anything. Everyone's card is valuable to them. It takes a reasonable mutual and trusting dialogue to rightfully access value propositions and make the right exchanges. Overleveraging your convenient edges, will definitely make you lose out sometimes.

It is therefore very important that we watch how we manage even our advantages with our partners. Since an edge in one domain, may not necessary be the same in everything, overleveraging your conveniences will only hurt you, because you cannot possibly have an edge in all that there is out there. The transient nature of these edges, base on our overheated business environments, diminishes the strength of trump cards with time. Such volatilities make them meaningless with time. Time is not still, and chance can happen to everyone.

The Geopolitical Environment in which Free Market Capitalism thrives Best

The maturity of business, takes time and patients. So long as you have a breathing space. Even in thin air, it is worth sticking with it. I say so because the events that usually catapults most businesses into high gear, are mostly unpredictable, though in can be discerned sometimes with careful attentive focus on the business environment.

The business environment transcends economics. It usually permeates almost all socio-cultural elements. The most prevalent of them, being the one most close to the governance of the state. This is so, because there is a fiduciary responsibility on the part of the governance bodies, to ensure fairness in commerce and also protect the safety of the general population. This process takes a dive into politics, which brings different coalitions together to access the best choices based on the interests of their constituencies, which constitutes their electoral caucus.

Due to the diversity of interests of the various coalitions which are filtered through by the demographic elements of the constituencies, there are often conflict of interests which are often settled by their hybridization through the shuffling of paramount interests to both sides, making the right concessions. There are often issues that are debated and often solved amicably. However, in most important high tension issues, consensus is often bought with equally valuable trading of interests. The value of such interests is often resolved through heated debates that sometime if not carefully resolved, could end in a dog fight. The good thing though is that somehow things get done through the superior negotiation skills of the legislative bodies, and also their insights in the constitution of the respective geo-political sovereign system.

      The constitution is simply a guideline, which determines the boundaries and permissible government actions and the authority of the legislative bodies. This legislative process is not a walk in the park, yet when it is all said and done, the constitution is amended when necessary, and the related bill is sent to the administrative body, the head of which is the president.

Some legislative bodies are flat, whiles others are hierarchical. An example of the latter is the legislative body in the USA. The first house is the congress with the senate on top of it. After a careful review of a bill, the congress votes on it, and passes it along to the senate. We often say you have to check your work before a final closure. For example if a surgeon cuts open a patient and perform a transplant. There are instruments that are used for the process. These are counted before the process begins. The count is necessary only to ensure that nothing is left in the body before it is closed. To make sure everything adds up, you always have to check your work.

The senate therefore, checks the work of the congress before in goes to the administrative body for the president to also review with his staff, and finally put his endorsement on it. Once finally endorsed, it became a law which then goes to the judiciary to be process finally into the law books.

As simplistic as I have described, it is not so simple, but for a layman this explanation will suffice. It gives enough insights to understand how it is all done. The above system described is called democracy. The power of the legislative body and the administrative, are all continent on their ability to convince their constituencies that they are their best represent in the process called an election.

It is simply a chance for all to exercise their power endowed by their citizenship rights to choose who best represents their interest.

To the prospective leaders, it is just a marketing and sales process. You have to put yourself and ideas in front of majority of your constituents, and make sure they remember what you stand for in the day of the election. If it resonates with many, they may give you their power and proxy to represent them.

This is necessary because there is no building that can pack the entire population to debate and make decision. Also if history thought us nothing, during the funeral of the Great Julius Caesar, which William Shakespeare beautiful described. There is often an element of fickleness in the collective minds of a mob.

Two speakers, speaking serially to the same mob, yielded both empathy and dissention, at almost the same time. The difference was who well explained the interests that resonated with the mob. The truth however is not so easily discerned, yet in others, cheer eloquence of rhetorical and oratory superiority, blind side lots of people. It is therefore more effective and efficient for a fewer representatives from the masses to decide based on the interest of their constituents.

One will then ask what this has got to do with business. The business environment and all its economic element and dynamics are guided by administrative bodies that are authorized by legislation, to ensure fairness in commerce, and consumer safety. This role puts them in an advocacy position for both consumers and businesses.

The responsibilities as described create both friendly and adversarial positions with conflicting tenets and interests. The resolutions of such pertinent issues, which may be restrictive to business sometimes, become quite contentious. I do not think a detailed description of the resolution process is necessary for our purposes. All I would like to say to this end is that, it will serve us better, if a systemic collaborative approach is taken to reach the most harmonized solutions in such instances.

Another way, the legislative process affects business, is the rights the constitution gives it citizens or immigrant population, usually called residents, be it permanent or temporary. These rights need to be protected. The most important of these are the freedom it give them to own property, and also use it at will, for whatever purposes suits their interest, which is socially acceptable.

For instance, owning a boom box does not necessary mean you have the right to blast in every ones ears. You may however have the right to use it at will, yet must be socially responsible. The freedom to use ones property for their own interest and the interest of other social causes are also permissible within socially acceptable and legal boundaries.

It is these rights and freedoms that often motivate people with high affinity for "freedom" to work hard to achieve the related resources that affords them those freedoms. This inner motivation drive people to think hard, work hard, and be patient enough to nurture the fruits of their labor.

This process may have inherent risks, some of which are manageable and others aren't. Manageable or not, risks are indispensable. Over analyzing of risk however are good and bad. The explanation may be apparent to many, but too much of everything is not always the best. It is even so, because uncertainty can never be fully absorbed, no matter what or how hard you try. Sometimes after a very meticulous and thoughtful examination of apparent and perceived business risks, it is just prudent to mitigate what you can, and manage the rest as time and flexibility affords.

Most often than not, the perceived risks disappear in thin air, and never land anywhere in any tracks. The uncertainty will just create an anxiety that often undermines your productivity, which at hind sight never shows up. It is always better to work harder, think harder and give it your very best. The rest is always in my experience, up to God, given the luxury of time and life. There is a lot more in the geopolitical environment that may not be necessary to talk about, since its relevance to business may not have much correlation to do with business returns.

With a good understanding of the political and economic environments which are most relevant to one's industry, it is easier to understand where the tide is going. It is very good to know, because you cannot be successful in business, leaning on the opposite direction of the tide within your industry or be blindsided by it.

The other side of the political system described above is the judiciary, which extend beyond the courts. It seeks to maintain the peace and civility needed to create the appropriate environment for business to thrive and do well. It also protect consumers who themselves are citizens, families and children to ensure a peaceful environment. Such an environment is needed to seek the ultimate wellbeing and happiness, which is a right for all who dare to do well for themselves. Be it an individuals, families or businesses, it is the aggregation of all of their activities, which finally gravitates to the macro elements of economics.

I believe Mr. Gates sort his happiness and well being by pursuing his own passions and dreams. It was the freedom that the constitution of the UNITED STATES OF AMERICA afforded it's citizens, and the protection given by the judiciary, that created the right environment which gave him the confidence to succeed. I believe such freedoms are what will afford the whole world a superior opportunity cost, in the pursuit of our overall ultimate end, happiness and wellbeing being the most paramount. This I believe is what all activities of economics seek to gravitate towards.

Capitalism therefore is the best choice, even if not adapted in its entirety. I also believe, most successful businesses all over the world, and their entrepreneurs, including Sir Richard Branson, and my own brother, Edmund Poku, who was trained in Columbia University in New York City became so, because of such philosophical inclinations.

I am saying all this because even in the remotest parts of the world, like Ghana, which Edmund's business is domicile, the same freedoms, coupled with the gems of free market capitalism, yield the same results anywhere.

The judiciary is the system of government that provides the requisite protection for both Businesses and Consumers. To this end I think it is enough for our purposes so long as the geopolitical business environment is concerned.

The Consumer markets

The consumer markets are simply the platform where both consumers and suppliers meet to exchange value. The value exchanged depending on the size of the market may be simple or very complex. When these markets extend beyond an individual sovereign nation, it creates the international business environment. These markets provides the opportunity for all to show their value in exchange for the appropriate rewards, which in this case could be either money, or anything of equal value as mutually agreed by both parties. These rewards are a way of saying thank you to each other, in business. The thank you is just to encourage you to do more, and solve more problems. This thank you then becomes the tool you need to do more in appreciation. This may have selfish inclinations. The expectations inherent in the minds of the partners, who are your consumers, are equally selfish. The intent is just for you to do more to help solve problems; with the gifts God has endowed you with, which is different for everyone.

It is therefore very crucial that the market place where such exchanges of value are done, should be free as Mr. Alan Greenspan has always been preaching so hard. I think with his level of insights as to how these things work; he is who our itching ears have to gravitate towards. I believe what he says, coupled with the other entire great economist out there, including the head of the British Central Bank, as well as all their global contemporaries in the world, matching so hard together lifting high the banners of free Market Capitalism should be taken seriously.

Anything free, and truly free in reference to such markets, is what gives the right momentum and accelerated pace to make things work the way it should, or at least designed to work. The requisite outcomes, if left to work that way, will perpetuate the ends we have so well dreamed to gravitate towards, our happiness and wellbeing. I believe so because; there is not much variability in the anatomy and physiology, of humans. It is the flexibility that the gems of free market capitalism afford all mankind, in the stage we exchange our value is what makes individuals and countries achieve such ends. Free Market Capitalism therefore will provide all, a superior opportunity cost to ensure that true happiness and wellbeing as compared to the other doctrines at the polar ends, such as communism.

Competition is a dog fight, yet that is just how it's done. However its workings, free of manipulations, will serve everyone better. If we all pay attention to these things, not only in words, but in deed as well, I believe the world will be a much better place. In the new world we are not so familiar with, I am confident that the natural working of a free local or global markets with capitalist inclinations, coupled with a systemic integrative thinking approach to problem solving, will definitely serve us better than any other known system.,

Let us not wait till we are too far along the way to realize that we left our most formidable tool behind, which I believe is free market capitalism. It may be too late to come back for it, if we go too far. Especially, far enough to make it difficult to trace our tracks back to it. Anything left in the dust, may or may not get eaten by the maggots, but even if you find our way back, it will be up to chance.

I say so because, like John Bunion, too much of a clutter will make the journey more difficult than we need. I say so because it will complicate the journey with lots of opposing frictions, which may decelerate the momentum, or bring it to a halt with unnecessary and wasteful dissipation of energy.

It is therefore very critical that we do not over leverage any such conveniences to perpetuate our own demise.

The financial markets

Both the formation of businesses and the operation of a matured one take some form of capital infusion. On the part of the consumers whose needs businesses serve, it takes their ability to pay for needed services and products.

For small businesses, the consumer banks are often the ones that serve the communities and provide business loans to those entrepreneurs who have such needs. Some of these loans are collateralized with assets most of which are relatively less liquid. Others are non-collateralized loans. The latter however often tends to be a bit expensive than the former.

After a review of your business proposal, if it makes sense to borrow at the offered leverage cost, which is often accessed by the respective interest rate the bank gives, it will be ok to go for it. If not, you keep searching. It is definitely not too wise to borrow at a rate that gives you a lesser rate of returns than your projected returns on your proposed investment or project. A superior return with enough margins for you to either break even or make a bit or a lot of profit, is a safer alternative than to borrow at a loss.

It is therefore important to give enough room as conservatism and flexibility can afford you. Planning without the appropriate contingency buffers, may create some brutal realities in business, that may not necessary be to your liking, or even force you to close shop depending on your cash flow and reserve capacities.

For relatively large businesses, to conglomerates that need a much bigger capital to manage their business operations, different instruments are accessible to raise cash, in addition to commercial bank loans. Some of these are bonds and equity stokes. There are any other instruments, but will just explain these two. For a deeper explanation of these instruments, I will recommend that one pick up a good book that is dedicated to the financial markets, with a much more detailed explanation of its inner workings.

A bond is simply borrowed cash from these financial markets, whiles an equity stock is a way of bringing more people into the business to invest their money as absentee owners. This means they may not have direct control over the day to day operational activities of the business.

Their influence however depends on the voting rights on major business decisions and policies the amount of their stocks gives them. The executives of the business are independent in their decision making, but are governed by the board of directors who have the fiduciary responsibility of making sure the cash and other resource are used responsibly, and not willfully abused.

They also make sure the appropriate executive body is in place with the right skills, insights and good mix of integrity and guts to make the appropriate decisions, and also manage well the requisite actions to make sure excessive waste is avoided, and most importantly the owners are reasonably rewarded with the right returns on their investments.

There are two major types of equity stock. One is called preferred stock. This give its owners a little bit of an edge in the distribution of returns permitted by the company by-laws and also authorized by the board. The other which is common stock, unfortunately, is last in line for such distributions of returns.

These markets where such instrument floats are called exchanges. An example of which is the New York Stock exchange. There are some indexes that help to guide the tempo of these markets. One is the Nasdaq Composite Index, and another the Dow Jones Industrial Exchange.

Nasdaq, mostly have the affinity for technology stocks with a bit more volatility, while the Dow is much more conservative, with less volatility relatively. The variability in volatility per exchange depends on a lot of factors most of which are both environmental and economically discerned. The uncertainty of these market dynamics makes it very emotional sometime when one feels the tide is against them. I am not going to go much further, but just to give you a little taste of how businesses raise funds or capital to ward off uncertain business tensions or finance other growth or innovative projects with immediate or future benefits to the company. The banks that deal with these exchanges are called investment banks, while the ones that most consumers and small business often interact with are called consumer banks.

The normal operations of business sometimes meet some uncertainties along the way. These risks may come from different sources. I cannot exhaust them here, but a few are usually caused by supply chain issues, especially for companies whose supply chain models have no built in redundancies, with a high reliability index. It can also be caused by catastrophic events like flooding, fire, and theft.

Some of these risks can be insured to avoid serious catastrophic losses in case they happen. Insurance help to indemnify the respective entities to avert any such serious consequential current and future loses, from respective insurable risks. There are also elements in insurance that help mitigate such business pains. Insurance and banking are highly regulated, and often under the same administrative government body. I think much more is not needed to get the picture I am trying to present regarding the financial markets that businesses rely on for both capital, and also a repository for excess cash. They also help in business transactions like mergers and acquisitions and a lot more other complex business financial transactions that makes both local and international businesses thrives well. It is the main engine that thrusts more liquidity into both local and international commerce, and also helps manage insurable business catastrophes, for indemnification purposes.

Convenience

For the most part, convenience depends on culture. For instance in Ghana, where I grew up and had my early start in life, we enjoy most of our basic staples with our hands. For most of them, such mode of eating is the most convenient. "Fufu" and "Ampesi" are a few examples. Though it does not hurt to use a spoon to eat them, it is not the most convenient way to fully enjoy them, especially "Fufu".

In most Chinese cultures, their staples are mostly prepared with rice. They also enjoy their delicacies with the chop sticks. In the USA, most dinning is done with the folk, spoon and knife. This is also the most convenient way of enjoying meals, though the hand creeps in some times, with some hard to cut pieces of meat. Though I have described three way of eating, the most convenient mode, depends on the culture from which they come from.

Convenience therefore afford you the most comfortable and efficient way of getting things done. There are so many things that make businesses convenient to operate. These business conveniences are many, and sometime complex to manage. Some of the most obvious things that make businesses convenient are cash and cash equivalents. When it is your own, we call it personal capital, and when you borrow from the bank or others, a loan. Borrowing money to earn a superior return on investments is called leverage.

When you manage to get enough of leverage to help you in your business, it works well. When you borrow too much than you can naturally afford, we often say in business, that you have over leveraged. Such over leveraging of business conveniences often can spell its doom. It is therefore very important that one borrows just enough for optimal business operations. Overleveraging of convenience can easily spell your doom.

In business negotiations, all parties come with their assumed trump cards. It may be a trump card in their imaginations, but to others it may not even worth a JACK. These cards, especially those that give a good business edge are also business conveniences. Naturally all negotiations have some inherent tensions; all parties try to leverage their relatively apparent conveniences. Everyone stretch as far as they can, to improve their assumed value.

It is though worth noting, that the elasticity of anything is not infinite. It you overstretch anything beyond its elastic threshold; you increase its propensity to break. The overstretching or over leveraging of such business conveniences more often than not, are more detrimental to business. It is therefore more prudent not to over leverage business conveniences beyond reasonable thresholds. In a capitalist environment, of which business if one of its essential pillars, it is always better to air on the side of conservatism, without overleveraging anything irrespective of short term benefits.

The speed of delivery of products within its natural cycle, gives an edge in the market place, especially for new and innovative ideas. This convenience can be a very good thing for business. That is why I said in the beginning that it is a gem and a menace. An early start in the market place often helps in capturing a bigger piece of the pie. It is therefore a good thing to leverage. A thoughtless or careless rush to the market with a product just to win a bigger piece of the pie is also very risk.

    The risk sterns from the chances of some production negligence that can also be very costly at the back end. Such convenience overleveraging will do more harm than good. Again it is therefore always better to leverage such nuances with great caution and speed where necessary. There are so many business conveniences that can be leveraged to improve business bottom lines, however over leveraging of such conveniences will do more harm than good, either for a consumer or a business.

Over leveraging of Convenience at the Micro Economic Level

At the micro-economic level there are a few major elements. These are Business entities, and consumers as has already been explained. Also the respective resources needed to produce the products to the markets, where consumers and businesses interact to exchange value. The major elements therefore are the markets, business entities, and consumers as well as the financial markets that serve both their leverage needs and repository for excess cash.

I will start with the consumer. To consume is just to use something, especially things that meet their individual needs. For example, nutritional needs, clothing, shelter, Transportation and so on. Our freedom to afford such needs is contingent on our financial freedoms, which depends on the value of our wealth, some of which are liquid whiles other aren't. Most times, for most people, their needs outweigh their resources.

To afford them the most value for their money, they have to make an individual or group decision, on how they joggle their resources, matching them with the needs that afford them a superior opportunity cost.

Most often, there are immediate and long term needs that get our resources stretched exhaustively, and sometimes exhaust our financial resource capacities. Depending on the urgency of the need, extra cash is often borrowed to meet such needs. Borrowing money is a convenient way of meeting such needs. Yet the ability to pay back has to be skillfully accessed with good projections.

Sometimes, the projections get off a bit, making it difficult to miss payments. However, if one borrows beyond perceived projected future capacities to pay back, then that convenience is overleveraged. It is therefore very critical that we access our ability to pay back such loans before we even ask for them, especially for durable and nondurable consumables that are not essential to life. It is ok, if you can afford them, yet to over leverage such convenience, is however not the most prudent way to live.

It is always better to manage ones ends well within their means, though there is nothing wrong with affordable luxuries, if you are so richly endowed. To over leverage only to rub shoulders with the Jones's just to be a "wonabe", I think may be just not prudent. I would say that a "wonable" can also be, but not necessarily at Neman Marcus, or Harrods.

Nothing wrong with Neman Marcus or Harrods, but to overstretch your pocket to just enjoy the coziness of their environment including their beautiful art work and chandeliers, may not be the best way to spend your hard earned money. You only take your merchandise with you, which may not even have the label of the store. The same merchandize with the same label, can sometimes be purchased at Marshalls, T J Max and many other discount stores, or Outlet Malls.

Sometimes with a little patience you can get it at the last call Neman Marcus Outlets on sale, on top of the original lesser prices at such outlets. With an over stretched budget, Wal-Mart can serve you even better and give you less stress, or K Mart.

You can get seemingly expensive stuff for much less than it is perceived if you shop right. B Js, Costco and their likes, can even afford you much cheaper jewelry with a better value than some of their competitors. Joseph A Bank may seem expensive, but not so expensive in season, if you have a bit of patience. It is therefore not very practical to rush with the Jones's at the front end of the fashion cycle, and give yourself a ton of headache and stress. Missing payments may give you more headaches in the long run, which will stifle your financial freedom even further.

At the business entity level, it is a bit more complex than the consumer level, which only constitutes serving an individual or family. A business entity often juggles much more than that. It usually joggles, and ascertains the right mix of labor, material, technology, and capital that can afford them the best returns.

Efficiency in the process, helps improve your odds, though it take a lot of diligent hawks eye to eventually squeeze the most juice out of s seemingly rocky looking pies. The process is not that easy, simply because the management of such complex processes may have some inherent risks some of which can slip no matter what you do. Risks in general, can never be fully absorbed. It is therefore important to plan to absorb some of such apparent and perceived risks, and hedge them well. I think the most difficult of these resources to joggle is the human resources. Not because they can talk back, but it take a lot to get the best out of them. Empowering, inspiring and motivating them depend on the individual things that give them the most kick.

The aspect of managing ones skill inventory, I believe should be a collaborative engagement between employees and employers. With the overheated dynamics of technology and market volatilities, individuals as well as businesses lose their edge quickly. Learning continuously therefore is the order of the day. Slouching too much will not serve either the employee or employer so well.

The need for skill upgrade, which is a very critical element of productivity, can only be possible if you have the requisite skills, as well as a good understanding of related theories regarding your industry domain.

With salaries shrinking even if you have a job, and the current inflationary trends which keep the salary trailing behind inflation, it will not be fair to ask someone who is struggling even to buy diapers for their children, to be solely responsible for his or her continuous education.

It is very convenient to shift business expenses out as much as affordable. Yet the overleveraging of this convenience to improve our returns, disregarding things like affordable employee educational expenses, is not the best, especially in industries with low employee turnover. Reason being that it is counterproductive to the bottom line we are working so hard to push up. Too much of that could even get the bottom to fall.

Sometimes all it takes is Tylenol to cure a simple headed so one can come to work again. This is not so expensive, yet if that is to be shared between bread and butter, most people will take a day off because they are entitled. May be, drinking water and sleeping may cure the same headache, that could have been treated differently and quickly with two pill of Tylenol in a first aid box at work. This can be applied in so many other business decisions. Sometimes we just over leverage our affinity for profit, forgetting that labor is even more critical than the material we handle with such caution. A fair and a well balanced mix of all these conveniences will serve all well.

It is always better to find a harmonized solution rather than the most efficient. I say so because, technology has served us well, but its gems for superior efficiency have also made many broke. This may not sit well with a lot of business owners. It is always good to make the best and the most buck out of our capital and resources, but the most efficient supply chain and productive systems often undermined the markets they serve.

Consumption is the ultimate goal of why we produce, however we do so for a market segment, which comprise of people just like those technology squeeze out of the labor markets. The optimum technological advantage is not always in the superior efficiency it can provide alone. We have to have as an industry, a good mix of labor, technology and guidelines our humanities domains afford us, with science. Over stretching either will just eventually undermine the purposes for which they are originally intended. Overleveraging such production conveniences alone, I believe will undermine the very markets, they are suppose to serve, squeezing the pie even further creating, overheating competition. It is therefore very important that the right mix of ingredients is shuffled in the production process, which seeks to maximize return. Over leveraging anything is not the best in many spheres of life.

The basic economic models have at the macro level aggregate demand and supply curve. The dynamics of these curves depend on a lot of things; the paramount on the consumer side is the ability to pay. The question is with what, depending on the rate of unemployment. It is therefore to seek and manage our ends well in a harmonized way, not necessary in the most efficient. Such outcomes may be great in the short term, the longevity of any successful endeavors as Mr. Buffet often say, is due to prudent insightful wisdom that do not undermine itself, though this is my paraphrase.

Too much stress on the efficiency factor has lots of short term recompense for individual entities struggling to survive, or even do so well. However, shrinking pies due to lack of affordability by many in your local or even international markets will only make the dog fight more vicious. A harmonized solution will help well. This is a business issue which needs critical evaluation and examination. It is so since it is the market place where the most buck is made, and made from families and individual's ability to pay.

Recessions and economics booms and bust, often come as a result of the un-harmonized mix of these ingredients in our quest to perpetuate our individual ends, which for most businesses, return on their investments. It is not so prudent to squeeze too much blood out of the market place without any plan to resuscitate. An anemic market do not serve anyone well. Any system, that is not renewable with short and long term strategies towards sustainability, will eventually gravitate to its own extinction. Renewability, though hard to achieve, will be ok for all. I will say then that overleveraging any business advantage too much, will undermine our own existence and business success. This is so, because the elasticity of any substance has a limited threshold, which is definitely not infinite.

Emotional short term decisions that often lead to economic booms and busts, do not only serve businesses adversely, but society at large. Our rush for the gold often undermines our patience and needed diligence to plan well and execute well. One of the reasons why I like Mr. Buffet is that, he does not throw either the dice or dots, in invents and issues, which are complex and inherently very unstructured and uncertain. He has proven that thoughtful evaluation and planning is better than a careless rush for anything.

He spent time to be an apprentice of the best of the best. With humility he learnt a lot, before he perfected even the very best, which have served him so well. I like him and his pals not only because they have money, but the purposes of their pursuits, and relentless determination, tenacity and focus, is what is mind bugling to me.

Though it is not so easy to make money, it is relatively more difficult to pursue a noble cause with superior noble intentions that are most often bigger than us. Convenience, like honey, may be sweet shortly, yet too much of sugar can get you obese or even an ugly metabolic syndrome related medical indication, which will not serve you so well in the long run.

The financial markets are where businesses borrow money to do business especially when there are liquidity shortages which the various business initiatives require. Borrowing money to make money is call leveraging as has been explained. The most prudent way to leverage is to do it in a way that will afford you some reasonable profit or returns on your investments. Therefore, your rate of business returns should be in much excess of your borrowing rate. The margin is what you typically finance your operations with, and still make some buck. If the flip side is true on paper, or much less conservative, it may be an irrational leverage.

Too much of over leveraging will not serve anyone well, no matter the short term advantages, they present. It is the same for businesses and individuals. Therefore, borrowing too much to pay for non essential needs that can be avoided may not be prudent, either in the short or long run. Overleveraging in business, an economy or even as an individual, just create financial stressors which often do not serve anyone well.

There are too many business conveniences which often produce some advantages. However these conveniences have to be well managed, in our pursuit of our ends. Overleveraging often do not give us long and sustainable solutions. The elasticity of any material is not infinite. Over stretching anything will not serve anyone well, in life and in business.

It is also not the best way to manage our economies. Its booms and busts though cannot be avoided, yet can also be averted or mitigated, with thoughtful and prudent choices, decisions and actions.

Over leveraging of Convenience at the Macro Economic Level

In a life time, most people witness good and bad times economically due to adverse impacts of poor economic cycles. These cycles are called recessions, and with a grievous intensity, a depression. They are sometimes unavoidable, yet can carelessly be triggered by the overleveraging of economic connivances.

The recent global economic bubble, associated with the over leveraging of the real estate market in the USA, and its related financial instruments moved shock waves all over the globe, with a tsunami strength, which almost crippled most economies globally.

The over leveraging of related conveniences both by the banks and consumers alike was to be blamed. Unfortunately both the consumer banking markets as well as the investment banking with the insurance and re-insurance industry were all not spared of the catastrophic consequential financial risk and loses.

The overleveraging by the consumer was simply over speculating. This I believe was also facilitated by the easy availability of leverage to finance such a gambling expedition. I say so jokingly only because I believe the apparent motivations were not quite rational. Such irrational exuberance often lean more to such dismal outcomes.

The irrational capital infusion from such overleveraging sparked a big fad. This phenomenon triggered a wave of inflationary pressures that got the real estate market so over heated. As we all well know, any overheated balloon will bust eventually. So a bubble busting is not a surprise.

I will therefore caution that, there is no easy way to succeed in anything. Just do not be fooled by anyone who tells you, throw a dice and become a multi millionaire. In short, the inclination of such a great number of people making such speculative judgment really bugs my mind. Mr. Warren Buffet has always been preaching about being thoughtful and diligent in inventing, especially with a long term horizon in business that offers sustainable returns.

The main culprits of the dome, were not only the consumers and their respective banks. The entire financial sector was intricately affected globally. All these were triggered by overleveraging the modeling of the instruments which were real estate backed derivatives.

With the apparent collaterals busting, the value of the instrument quickly diminished sending a big shock wave all over the other investment vehicles that carried some of its weight. This brought a lot of companies, in the financial sector down, the likes of Goldman's, and Burstein. In fact all or most of the big banking and insurance conglomerate were almost brought down to their knees.

The ones with deep grips and much depth in the economy, deemed to be too big to fail, were saved by direct government intervention, and a systematic infusion of public capital into the financial markets, which is termed quantitative easing. JP Morgan Chase Bank and City Group are examples of such affected institutions. The adverse impact of this issue affected many businesses and consumers worldwide, big and small. Such overleveraging of conveniences in business and in life mostly does not serve us well in the long term.

Overleveraging of convenience and our state of health

Obesity is one of my passionate endeavors and I hope together it will be conquered. There are many factors that have caused the rate of its accelerated growth in recent times. I would however like to share a few things about how overleveraging of convenience can even push as faster to our grave.

I am not going to talk too much about the formation of obesity and what factors drive its co-morbidity. The over leveraging of convenience associated to obesity, amongst others, is tightly associated with our sedentary life style. Often, the most convenient way of doing things are the methods that are efficient and effective in dealing with the issue at stake. The effectiveness of a method though is relative. The level of relativity is pertinent to the number of stakeholders involved and their respective interests.

A unilateral decision or method, which harms no one, but suits ones interest is ok. In situations where multiple interests collide, a hybridized form is usually better. It is more prudent to collaborate and come up with a very harmonious solution which works well for everyone. This is so, because everyone's interest is important to them, no matter how trivial it may seems.

As I said before, the hand may be the most convenient tool for some delicacies in some cultures, whiles the sticks may be for others. The spoon also works well as well. The best convenient way of doing things for an individual is what works for them, depending of the circumstances and needs.

For an individual, regarding sedentary lifestyle and healthy living, the definition of convenience may have counteractive inclinations, with opposing effects. The reason is that, though it will be ok, to afford yourself some convenience by sparing the muscles from aching a bit, however, overleveraging a lifestyle that afford you too much of such conveniences, can be counterproductive "health wise".

To adapt solutions that undermine such ends as health, happiness and wellbeing are really irrational. The willful propagation of such intents are obviously not in the interest of anyone. It is always better to gravitate toward solutions that has multilateral interest, especially that which relates well with our goal of achieving our ends, such as a good state of health.

Obesity therefore, as we all know is a very serious issue to all humanity. It is very important that, in our quest for solutions, we seek those that gravitate towards our real intents and goals. Sedentary lifestyle therefore is not the best way of dealing with Obesity and related issues. It is therefore critical that we look well into the elements in our culture that, perpetuate such sedentary lifestyles and find the most effective alternatives.

For example, there are some nuances of our culture which need to be averted to help reverse the tide. Some of these issues may transcend the individual. For instance, the divorce rate in many cultures, which leaves children with single mothers, is often not the best. Some of these mothers are not so fortunate to have productive skills and resources that give them enough returns to help meet their financial obligations. As a result, they have to work two or more jobs, leaving their children behind televisions, limiting their choices to sedentary indoor life styles.

Growing up, we had to walk a lot of miles, play in open spaces, and often eat at home. These activities and its apparent outcomes were quite visible to all. I do not remember a lot of my friends who had childhood obesity problems, though there were a few. All I am saying is that, it is better to always make sure; we seek ends that re-enforce our systemic goals.

Besides the issue of divorce, health inequities are very closely related to our socio-economic status. Globally, this has been recognized by many world leaders, including our most noble and Honorable President George W. Bush, and also Professor Jeffery Sacks, an economist at Columbia University in New York City.

It was apparently their recognition of global wealth inequities that influenced their passions to support the global initiative to improve the wealth and well being of many around the world to bridge the Global wealth inequity gab.

This noble initiative which is called the Millennium Project, of which poor countries like Ghana, and many others are beneficiaries, are working so hard to make sure its goals are met, on time and within budget. The global wealth inequity, if properly managed, will help poor countries afford, clean water and many other amenities that can also help them manage the proliferation of infectious diseases and more.

All our socio-cultural and anthropological elements with their various systems and sub systems should be revamped accordingly to gravitate towards such healthy life styles, which can help prevent many related chronic diseases.

The best way to enjoy our success is within a peaceful environment. Peace however, is not achieved by the overstretching of either the truth or lies. It only works with our inclination toward peace itself. A little stretching may be appropriate. Yet even with peace, over leveraging either is counterproductive.

I may say that, we can effectively achieve most of our economic goals in an atmosphere of peace. It is such and only thus, will we all enjoy our piece of the pie that our hard work affords us. Obesity may be very complex to understand, but in all its complexities, taking little steps at a time gravitating toward solutions that are systemically and collaboratively design, will get as further along the way.

Conclusion

Capitalism has definitely come a long way. The journey has not been smooth, and the path has also been meandering. Through all its changes, and the dynamics of its metamorphoses, I am confident that in the onset of this new turn, into it biggest frontier, though called a village, leaving it behind will be one of the biggest mistakes posterity will regret from hind sight. Let us all pay close attention and make sure we do what is needed to foster the appropriate collaborative engagements that will hybridized all interests to avert the forces of aggression that can possibly undermine its noble courses.

We call it a village, and it is rightly so, because of technology which accelerated it momentum in recent times. Besides these, the late starters are also worth mentioning. The new wave of social media companies are also due some accolades. If not for them, we would have probably called it a city, making no difference as to those we live in today, though it is much bigger. To mentions a few, I will say: Facebook, LinkedIn, "YouTube", Twitter and all the rest of their contemporaries. For those who gave up a tone of free bytes for people to afford e-mails all over the world, I would say they also require the same; the likes of Yahoo, Google and their contemporaries as well.

Also the related technologies that made it all happen, which started with the hypertext markup language, then the .Net, Java and C and C++, not forgetting also the brain children of the early programs, the likes of the assembler, Fortran, basic, and Cobol which finally gave way to C, and the rest of the newer applications that demystified, computer programming. Also, all the related hardware vendors who also provided the platform on which transformational applications resides, as well as those that faithfully carried the bytes across the village. For all of those who also developed the related protocols that made the journey smooth along the wires, including AT&T, and Arcatel Lucent.

I know there are more to mention, some of which I have already, I repeated AT&T corporation here, a company that I am proud off, the same way we are all proud of our Alma Matters. We are proud because we learnt something from them. I will say thought the opportunity to work for them, and well as learn from them was invaluable and well appreciated.

For their recognition of my little efforts, I will also say thank you for being so thoughtful, for the scales don't even match. I think though that I should have given you a plaque, for the great opportunity you gave me. For all academic institutions that provided the skill and innovations that the journey demanded, also deserve some accolades.

For all those who worked tirelessly for the onset of the needed momentum of the industrial revolution, you all deserve a good handshake. I wish you could all wake up in your graves to see how far we have come. To such great leaders like General Eisenhower of the USA, and Sir Winston Churchill of the Great Briton, we will throw it in the air, in thanks given to the almighty to whom all blessings flow.

From the end of the world war two, to the onset of the League of Nations, which precipitated into the United Nations, we have came very far with this noble ideas of capitalism, but as I said before, all this hard work, may not mean much in an atmosphere of chaos. I am hopeful that we will all recognize that, and make the superior choice for peace, at least to afford ourselves the luxury of enjoying the fruits of our hard labor.

To this end I will mention at least, one past United Nations Leader in recent memory, that helped in his own rights to broker such needed peacefully focused collaborative engagements with many great nations, and formidable coalitions along the globe. Mr. Kofi Annan, I believe also deserves some accolades, though in his honor, he stand in the stud of all his present and past colleagues as well as subordinates.

Then to all who also risked much more of their lives in sacrificial ways to promote peace, that precipitated the needed environment, which I believe made Capitalism navigate the landmines so well to come this far. To all nations big and small, I believe we are not going to be "obese", yet there is a lot more room for growth for everyone.

Finally to those who worked tirelessly to keep our labor forces in good shape, starting from the World Health Organization, NIH, CDC and their international contemporaries, Hospitals, clinic and polyclinic all over the globe and the Komfo Anokye Teaching Hospital in Kumasi Ghana, which ones saved my life from an accident, which almost got my left arm amputated. To all of its likes around the world, in countries big and small, with their most noble health workers, I would say keep on hanging on.

Your passions, being in the direction of the tide for which all the forces and inner working of economics seeks to gravitate toward, which is our wellbeing and happiness for all, is close.

I will reiterate finally, that Business has a lot to do with the achievement of the needed resources that can greatly improve our odds. The atmosphere in which business thrives best, is an environment of peace. I therefore may throw a caution, that we all hold our breath a bit, though it is hard to do some times to give it a chance.

To this end, I would say may the providence of the divine guide us, as it did for its brain children of CAPITALISM, as we are ushering a new ERA yet unknown to mankind. We have had a few bumps, yet with the help of even the new starters like China, we managed them so well the most recent global turmoil. This example therefore shows that, if we all do well, it will be well for all.

I will finally end with a joke. This though is not to ridicule anyone or company. Upfront I will say it is about AT&T, a company that I am very proud of. I am ending with it because of a few lessons the world need to learn from the experience I am going to share.

At the onset of the telecommunication boom in the USA, there were giant telephony companies, the likes of; AT&T, with its R & D wing named after Mr. Bell, the brain child of the Telephone. The other rivals companies were, MCI and Sprint, all riding sweet oligopolistic markets. I said sweet in a funny way, yet such a market was needed, because of the apparent infusion of capital for the development of such a giant telecom infrastructure which has served us so well globally.

There came a time that the big bells had to divest themselves in smaller entities to avoid the conflicts of interest that will undermine the interest of its targeted consumers. The Mother Bell as we called AT&T divested itself into the Baby Bells, which became the local statewide telephony vendors, or intra-lata telephony vendors. One of the baby Bells that AT&T gave birth to was the South Western Bell Company.

There was a time that another cycle of divestiture became necessary, which caused it to divest itself again into AT&T and Lucent technology, which has now merged with the French Company Alcatel, giving its new name Lucent-Alcatel. I started my technology career at the Bell Labs which was in Holmdel NJ, which became part of the real estate of Lucent Technology.

During the tenure of our Honorable President Bill Clinton, there was another wave which was more customers favorable. The intent of Honorable President Clinton was to make sure competitive forces of a free telecommunication market help shape the pricing of its services.

This initiative, triggered a lot of competition in the market, which did exactly what was intended. As a young immigrant in New Jersey, having my mother and father home in Ghana at the time, my phone bill was much greater than my groceries bill for the month, trailing closely behind my rent.

Yet today, I can buy a $2.00 phone card to call anyone anywhere. Even better, the merger of voice and data which the advancements in telecommunication fostered to emerge gave way to the voice over internet protocol which has made possible free phone applications like Tango and others.

These trends has been kind to a lot of us, but was not so kind to the very company that started it all. Not that this outcome was by design, it is just some of the fate entrepreneurship fosters. For the good, the bad and the ugly, Capitalism is still a superior option, for its aggregate benefits globally cannot be compared to any better known good option.

This is just an example of how the inner working of Capitalism and its intricate market forces can help even a little boy originally from Ghana; communicate with my parents, friends and family on a free video conference, such as Tango.

The invisible hand of this powerful market dynamics was not so kind to the Mother Bell. However, one of its children saved the day, and gave it the respect and honor, and help it even maintain its original identity and name [AT&T], it would have been lost in history.

This message may be debatable in other sphere and domains in life, but I will just end here and leave that to individuals. Let us all incline our hearts toward peace, for it is such inclination itself that will lead us in the direction of peace. Overleveraged the truth or lies, as I have said already, gives conflicts a trump card, to undermine our stability. The benefit of rioting, only sooths our ego often, and leave us desolate.

Overleveraging the convenience of our perception of being right without making concessions for peace, will afford us only chaos. Such an environment, will only lead to our own demise. Empathy is often needed by all, to encourage needed compromises for accelerating the pace towards peace. Overleveraging the egos hunger is not normally the best. It ultimately undermines all positive goals and projected outcomes.

We therefore have to be very careful, in our pursuits of anything, and we have to leverage our cards well. For even beauty is in the eyes of the beholder. The two most important tolls we need to put in our arsenal or toll box, is in my opinion Capitalism and PEACE. Because the preeminence of the goals we are working so hard toward, cannot be achieve in the reverse. One should precede the other. What should lead, I believe is peace.

Capitalism and peace will afford us more than just luxury. It took the sacrifice of many to bring it this far. Therefore posterity demands, not even requires similar sacrifices, the purposes of which is more noble than the conveniences of any others, less purposeful.

www.ingramcontent.com/pod-product-compliance
Lightning Source LLC
Chambersburg PA
CBHW030743180526
45163CB00003B/900